The Powers that Be

J. S. CUNNINGHAM

The Powers that Be

LONDON
Oxford University Press
NEW YORK   TORONTO

1969

Oxford University Press, Ely House, London W.1

GLASGOW NEW YORK TORONTO MELBOURNE WELLINGTON
CAPE TOWN SALISBURY IBADAN NAIROBI LUSAKA ADDIS ABABA
BOMBAY CALCUTTA MADRAS KARACHI LAHORE DACCA
KUALA LUMPUR HONG KONG TOKYO SINGAPORE

© Oxford University Press 1969

*Printed in Great Britain
by the Bowering Press, Plymouth*

TO
My Mother
and
Jill my Wife
NOW, AND
Katharine Christopher
Simon Hamish
my Children
LATER
THESE INKLINGS

Acknowledgements

Acknowledgements are due to the editors of the following periodicals in which some of these poems first appeared: *Eboracum, Manchester University Poetry, New Statesman, North East Arts Review,* and *Times Literary Supplement.*

Contents

You may know	1
As under is	2
What grows up to the top	4
The world before us	5
Ice-bound	6
Thesaurus	7
Three, one, and now two	7
Concurrences	8
Fountain, Lake	9
Beggar my Neighbour	10
Under the axe	11
Amphibians	12
Dead Letter to Andrew Marvell	15
Park Benches	16
Museum Gardens	17
At the Wrestling	17
Sand ribbed	18
Nocturne, with Television	19
nelegy in a Suburban Churchyard	21
September Dusk: for Molly Bloom	22
My Daughter's Birthday	23
Come see	24
Television Show in a Pub	26
Undressing	27
Paradise Affirmed	27
Up in the where	29
North	30
Sick Visit	31
In the prompt afterwards	33
Reminded	34
Sometimes retrospection yields	35
Now Showing	36
Child's Play	37
Very Portent Impersons	38
Niet Wham	38
In War Time	39
So simply tapped	46
Far Cry	48
The Powers that Be	48
Philosophy	49
Home Thoughts from Toronto	50
Hello . . . Testing	54

> Mean while the Mind, from pleasure less,
> Withdraws into its happiness:
> The Mind, that Ocean where each kind
> Does streight its own resemblance find;
> Yet it creates, transcending these,
> Far other Worlds, and other Seas;
> Annihilating all that's made
> To a green Thought in a green Shade.
>
> Andrew Marvell, 'The Garden'

After we came out of the church, we stood talking for some time together of Bishop Berkeley's ingenious sophistry to prove the non-existence of matter, and that every thing in the universe is merely ideal. I observed, that though we are satisfied his doctrine is not true, it is impossible to refute it. I never shall forget the alacrity with which Johnson answered, striking his foot with mighty force against a large stone, till he rebounded from it, 'I refute it *thus*.'

Boswell, *Life of Johnson*

You may know

                        I cannot know
what it is to be you and
knowing it

I stand here in a forest of me
with a gale of my own
blowing it

this idiot charade
will not give way, try violence
try stealth

try to think into you, the louder
rhubarb rhubarb
goes my self

the marks I make on this glass wall
impede your try
to make me out

the certainties I have of you
are yours and others'
doubt

I keep you where I cannot
let you be, in downright
uproar in my head

skin-deep in swirls of falling
words, the live and
clamorously dead

deciduous reminders you
nor I could know us one
us two

were even all that could be, said
:while our astounded spirits
mutely run

clean through the brambled
self-sown forests bothly
one

gay, carnal, temporary
limpid, complicated
intimate

with what we know
                      we cannot know

As under is

its odd own
side of things

where pools and runs
of waterish dry flat light
merge wobble flicker
bounced
out of their element
voluble

or sibillant leaks
blob down from sodden
graves of miners
through the bricked
ferny roof of worked out
lead seams
dank with furry bluegreen
stalactite stamen
bloom

or goldfish
frozen stiff
a spiny curve
as if it had been turning
as the ice took
paper-weight hold
syntactical

or where the slithery
pothole corridor
reaches dead end
a dry-boned
smallish quadruped
articulated by
his curious posterity
waits in a glass box
in electric light
conjecturing how long
he lay until reconstituted
such a wiry tip-toed
sentence of death

or whale vertebrae
cryptically strung
along an iron rod
below the west end
of the cathedral's
chiselled grammar
awaiting the crack of
doom

:infant sayables
along the seamy permeable
undersides of words
!rejoice rejoice
below the throbbing fontanelles
down lost shafts, nervy corridors,
through icy membranes, jarring
linkages, ageless deposits—

inklings blobbing into
oddly recognizable
outlandish namesakes
whispering frightening asking
voice voice voice

What grows up to the top

to say so
folds off the rippled level
freakishly
green undersides of water
lily elephant lugs leaves

or keeps impending
way back across
lake edges in the mind
a rooted wavering
insistence, tendrilous

or gathers far behind
white lidded sideways eyes
on screwy duck heads
pondering back to front
the damp webbed brood green
yews whose hollow fullness
mythically screams
nothing out loud

:the truth is
sproutingly odd soggy
natural distinct alive
close to unsorted nowt like any
unsense or sense worth letting
grow to the top to say

The world before us

long before us
far and near before—

with pale blue ground haze
unapproachably
rising below the level elms
whose trunks close to
shine green live mouldy
edgeless
as animated flesh—

this world was
long-agog Lucretius his
onion: 'a sort of outer skin
peeled off the surfaces
of objects'

:bloom is both
dead and alive
an iridescent rabbit
flyblown in a filmy mist
of daisies

and it is this
eerie visibility
such bright entire
appearances
'whose impact scares the mind'

above all when as now
the whole world
is the look of it

rising up ghostly
to declare the clocks
have stopped

Ice-bound

sticky road bridge
smokes under stranger feet

an ether-needled
mossy railing
steams in last winter's sun

words long unsaid
sprout from dry crevices
of stone bridge arches
and vaporize in thin airs
catching next week's breath

hands all thumbs
jiggle free gnarled
igneous wedges of cold
weathered brick wall
and throw them into skidding
chuckling wobbles
over ice how thinly
sleep years deep

the mill weir pool
has frozen but for
wind-feathered estuaries
up to the brink
and there spills over
from two hundred years upstream

:we are outlived
by sparrows we remember
from before a single one
of them was born
singing as Pompeii set cold

as if none of this were
too vivid, edgy, strange
to simply celebrate
or what it is they do

Thesaurus

quote Time unquote which so to say
flies drags rebukes deceives
estranges kills forgets consoles
ticks dances pulses grieves

domesticated scapegoat for
anthropomorphic metaphor

and happens, too, like death love sleep
life hate—try permutation
:convenors of the fake profound
in image paradox equation

like Death is Sleep and Hate is Love
the eagle mateth with the dove
hey-nonny-no, tra-la

whereas unto the Self we cry
Be who I am, stay what you are,
will spirit glands integrity
blamed or exonerated, Me

though sometimes narcissistically
confused with God, whoever He

for instance light love otherness,
abstractions to the power of n,
no sooner superseded than
semantically born again

:all hail to language while it can
so muddle and illumine man

Three, one, and now two

evening people out of my
quiet window out of earshot

pause to say
in looking at a swan I too
would talk of with in words they use
to glass in from, look out at through

'how time runs by
as I said then—did you!'

behaving as the language means it to

just as it did when last not I
nor dwindling these stood there to try
using the words we
see through for
discussing with and of to hide
misgiving at that silent, cold

short-memoried, mute, fabulous
absurd bespoken dignity

implacable who rides our blood stream by

Concurrences

Slate-blue greenish purple silver gold
cacophony of shiny tinsel strips
streaming the fronts of Used Car lots

compose in a stiff sleety breeze
the fluctuating half-syllabic turbulence
of mountain water, lipping, memorizing

silted flats, down slate-veined
curved edges into slant-lit
pools dark under rooty mud banks, glinting

from which rise concrete cliffs, rain-runnelled,
overhangs—balconies, office windows,
coming alight with misty fluorescence

deepening the street awash with merging
oil-patch rainbows, unsyntactical
:and through the street
                    old woman, talking
quite loudly to herself, insistently

mouthing, fishily in their element
words, and as we pass she smiles
?half-crazed, as if I understand we share

a shining, calm, profoundly
consequential wisdom somewhere neither
deep nor shallow, now, then, here nor there

composed of far-fetched sayables
which only she can quite afford to
turn into, so greenly drowning, drowning

Fountain, Lake

Watery cool sunlight climbs
each talkative spurting jet
                    and spills
in splashy circlets altering
the shapes of thinking outwards to

a feel of words at edges where
the fountain pool builds to a dam
then runs and glints inventively
into green deep whose levels, gleams

half-lights and nervous tendrils
occupy my mind
              :and that seems why
out here insidiously chills me now
that not an idling stir

ruffles the lake, but just below
!ice, whose random fossil-veins
hold scraps of newspaper
one trade-marked carton, twigs

extravagantly itemized
by that sharp miser in the brain
lets nothing go, and steals upstream
his opaque fingerings of cold

Beggar my Neighbour

What is breath but wasted breath
now there has come to stay
this famished shadow at my side
to gnaw the joy away?

Rehearse a calm, defensive stance
can I, when in his head
I see my own skull split the skin
and feel it strike me dead?

Or stamp my feet for warmth, although
in mid-July I stand,
and blame the sharp October for
the cold hand in my hand?

I know he intercepts all men
in each man's aging form,
yet I to them and they to me
look unaccosted, warm.

Beside myself with fear of him
I scrabble deep in sand,
and in my throat I hear him say
I next to nothing stand.

Then with his eyes I see me beg
on my knees, whine and pray,
and if I turn, obsequious
he brings me on his way.

Breath is merely wasted breath
and half my gain is lose
unless I learn to laugh him out of
so much dying in my shoes.

Under the axe

               this chicken
lost its head
and flappingly gushed
up on the balustraded
willow pattern bridge

failing to discompose
delicate blue fronds
garden house fountains
sacrificial nooks
and a serene Confucian
thinking abstractly
of his dinner

while round him stumbling flew
inedible melody
in the belated name of all
alive and unplucked
flowers at the water's edge

from before Lethe and before
vegetarian Adam
Cain and all the killers
we have been

:and fell down twitching
on the butcher's concrete
in the beginning was

the bitter mutual need
of hot rare violated
flesh and that sweet
unheard elegist who sings
too late too late
the tears of things

idling on which
of all streams
the buoyant sensitive skilled
paper boat of our mundane
tenderness
drifts to the sleepy lake

Amphibians

Doctor Johnson, widower
remorseful
carnal, pious, frightened
keeper of deathdays

'depraved with vain
imaginations'
'disturbances of the mind
very near to madness'

although he seemed the uttermost
substantial notion
in the mind of Ghost

kicked a big stone
to show God's Irish socratery
that was that
and out there on its own—

irrelevance
repairing for a season
more hurt than was sustained
by such well-shod horse-sense—

'perhaps no human mind
is in its right state'.

Stella's kind steplover
dean of hell
dreamed apish Gullible
mad with reason

ashamed begetter
making sense to horses
private, shunning biped
feminine smell.

Nature's orphan
walking blind
beside 'the abyss of idealism'
clutched wall or tree

to keep him sensible of
ghostly reality

where he might lie down
in a trench to hear
the quiet breath of Lucy dead
below the twisted roots of fear.

Ledaean Alice, motherly
fearing the Red King
would catch cold
huddled on the grass asleep

was mocked by dunces
frightened in the dark
for thinking that her tears could mean
she was more than a sort of

play thing in his dream—
he, pseudonymous logician,
death's uneasy jester, chaste.

Riddling with Plato's virgin ghost
too late about the woman lost
who strayed across Apollo's lawn
tone-deaf to ghostly songsters
silver or gold

too mildly bored to yawn
at Marvell's ocean-mirror-gazing
circus animals

and languidly lay down
ignored by lofty Berkeley
and sweetly single-bedded
grave-digger Thomas Browne

who day-dreamed he could be
'content that we might procreate
like trees . . . without this
trivial and vulgar
way of union'.

Do such eccentric
half demented
lone mock turtles
between devil and sea

invent their fabulous
expedients, careful shells,
for what we rarely
dare admit to be

common extremity
the root of which
to love's indifference
is not philosophy but she?

'In brief, we all are monsters'
'great and true *Amphibium* . . .'

Dead Letter to Andrew Marvell

This is me on the outside looking in
with damp sand paling round my feet
as and when I look at them
upon this brink of alteration

>hands full of
>rust-veined spar ends, Ulysses'
>rope soles, crab claws drifted
>all the way back from Troy, drained
>empty of those loud lies

me looking through the mirror of
the mind, that ocean where each kind
confronts its unresemblance

>cat and cat-fish, horse and
>sea-horse, land-wife, sea-angel,
>sea-wife, angel . . . Helen
>flayed, sea-changed

slants and gleams
of consciousness

>on his mean own
>the shark sea-lawyer
>altering his improvident
>lean acres for the worse

ravening all that's made,
the mind, omnivorous in his green shade

Park Benches

A drowse of bees in tidy
wallflower beds
               the steady swerve
of ash-grey shadows on the lawn

:marooned by dusk, uneasily,
belated wish and reminiscence
pollinate the scented merge
of want and cannot on the verge
of tears.

The cripple runs, delirious,
a grey maid's chalk unyielded knee
cradles a child,
blind men stride through
the startling shrubbery,
hushed fantasies run wild.

Lilac deludes, the virgin borders
betray a failure of nerve,
grey seeps into each glazing face

nor can this brief community
of dream wish light and scent
invent a tactic to deflect
that stealthy
               screaming shadow
from their verge of fears

:on which we balance
walking past, sustained
only less totally than these
by such fantastical
rehearsed, expensive
daylight robberies

border raids, rope walks
vivid, half-disabling,
needy, improvident, wild.

Museum Gardens

Peacock screech
              the scorched air turns
bronze green blue glinting blue, all eyes
and swivels in the stirring
envy from these complicated human
ones and twos, hen-mesmerised
by his undilatory self-display:
I AM I who violates
at will and equally at will subsides.

Scores of lazy feather fishes
dither at gaze in his wide wake.

Leisurely fan-fold
              pert, he glides
past petalled cottons rippling on green
ocean floors in obscure tides,
past love-locked and onlooking twos and ones
constrained on bench and lawn to cry
their fork-tuned silent cry.

Ancient and intricate with wishes,
baffle-willed, unseasonal, opaque.

At the Wrestling

Crowd and its double crowded there
watching this epileptic
two-backed octoped
cut off from them, at bay

to howl scoff twisted
howl in ropes of noise
off which it bounded, two
-faced, fell and hurt itselves

then tore and split in raw
derision, one hurt half
cut off, all bleed, not able to
get up and walk away

:on which that other fell
and grew themself again, locked
knotted mauled, looked
blindly at its own grimace

:so loudly furtively approved
I grew to think it was
begetting us upon itself
on all of our behalves

:which did not agonize
that aping hydra watching, who
got up, stood, dwindled into half
and shook itself in bus queues

two by two

Sand ribbed

uplit clouds
as day goes out
night falling
risingly
a leisurely vague tide
shoreless
the horizon rising
hazing

:so much letting go
however peaceably the lake
glosses over

hearing peers
at lessenings which furtively
congeal

attention widening
the more shut in
it keens
in obscure wires
relinquishment
accumulating!

Each evening terrifying
like (but there was never
one) the first
(and each is partly
last)

fall rise
shoreless tide

while somewhere deep
a chilly full
stubborn buoyant
expectancy
half whispers
soon soon soon

Nocturne, with Television

It has taken half a winter's
        dank night walks
down past the cemetery loud
          with rheumatism—

trees root-deep in the
        extreme decencies
carpentry and linen (leaves drink
      men)
creaking and cracking in frost
        they have the edge on us
not to have to anticipate—

  to the ironically adjacent
     sewage pumping station
(that it should come to this)
  and the river
Great Mother Hydrogen Dioxide
   eternal conceptor
who evidently carries on
    some underground trade
in dogs 57 Varieties
   a seamy fluctuation
creaking and straining . . .

It has taken one and a half score
   years and five,
half my spanned allotment
   (*il faut cultiver*)
in this vale of pretty well
   every variety

to learn that man shall be outlived
    unwittingly
by dazzled goners with warm feet
   on sheep,
shining blue corpse-light back
   the light of the world
at half a score square
   glass inches and seven

keeping warm, at gaze
   in the bright mist of
other unpeople's palpable
   clarities
because they have no deepness of earth . . .

Too shallow, far too soon
   I shall be gone
more poor in spirit
   than the slow
lovers can conceive—

                they shall inherit
the rental card and the blackmail
            cereals advertisement
lest at any time they should
            see with their eyes—

taking my time para-metrically
            down through the cemetery
and the stations of the
            City Waterworks Board

my mouth dry with unholy
            thirst
and this ash taste
            of human incry they may never
mark learn inwardly
            digest

!Sunshine Breakfasters
            invincibly semi-detached
which is cosier than trying to
            cultivate roots
for heaven's sake

:roots only accelerate processes
            all the better to
drink you with

            whereas sheep

eat men slowly

nelegy in a Suburban Churchyard

Light worsens where I
(seemingly because I)
creepily, bat-webbed

brood on my brooding on
these downcast goners

        ALSO WIFE OF THE

fell guys
for some old chiseller's off-white
lies

        AT REST FELT SLEEPY
        date and place

HERE LIES
in seeping gathering clotting
umbrage, decent

        ALSO DAUGHTERS OF THE
        underneath ABOVE

who loom so seemly, damply round
time-serving
        in the need of
scything laughing sunlight and
fresh hair

September Dusk: for Molly Bloom

Thinking how furtively night rises
restive in fields where summer lay
slack-limbed, all groin and nippled
hillock, rifled by
hands, eyes, and her incendiary
fantasies

        :and images like these
to keep the cold out of my

:sudden I saw, still see
flat on her back, rived over stocking tops
with her crouched rider flaring up
the swollen darkness through her

    :wise as you
she (someone) open wide as night

:and I who felt my wick light
at their blaze, gawped at, darkening
offstage, their
        Yes is Why

then walked on, languaging
their rage: blind energy's aping
celebrant in poetry's glass cage.

My Daughter's Birthday

May looking fall
never less gently on you
than tonight I see
breath-taking sleep
rising behind your eyes
with wholesome ghosts

and a minority
of bogeys exorcised
easily, more or less, by trust
or some achieved
or, rarer, careless
adult kindness, if and when
forthcoming

    :being, this,
only my whole wish
full of the sense
itself excites, being whole,
that it should nor can come
to realization.

Men soon enough
will eye you with such
rifling violent congested
welcome stares

as I today had thrown
at one who turned
!too young, let fall
negligent, not on me,
eyes a few years
only less innocent
than yours, not
interested even had she
seen, guessed, heard
the silent, strident

shallow truancy
of this inconstant, loyally
insolvent heart
which with the constant gap
!twenty odd years
between us widening
keeps capable, feeling you grow,
of simplifying joys

less frequently, more carefully,
grows wholesomer
as its own worse ghosts rise

:each gentler impulse hurt
by sore routine atrocity;
dependances left out to rust;
bright with my belatedly
whole kindnesses
my father's old entire live eyes.

Come see

—at least he is all right
running across the bumpy ground
as if the world were flat—

that water all run out!

:none of us had quite thought
he'd been too quiet far too long
too near the river swollen in our heads
too deep with daydream drownings—

hot noon, sweet perverse inertia—

while he had simply strayed
back round the fisherman's caravan
and kicked a bucket just to see

!out flopped all spiny flicking
wriggle squirm loop in tangled grass
live minnows kept for bait
that caught him whole for swollen
moments puzzlingly disastrous

:to be picked up, put back
(I angry, blind, relieved,
exhilarated, whole,
but vaguely mesmerized by all
that worst that had not
yet, at least, happened)

!over,
and all to dread and wait for
over again, too deep too ticingly
blendingly irrigating live with die

with drowsy will-falls bright
young wilfulness, with trance
vertiginous delight
on brinks where worst
is far too close to wished
however sensibly we try

Television Show in a Pub

Drum stutter
                gasp and flare of brass
Light swims and angles
                      Dim
                          Now
                              Glare
:among a carpentry of tilts and screens
look at their
            thighs pose flex flicker
how they
        in a slick routine
                        Dissolve.

She
    I bet she knows how to
shimmies
          an argent sheath
                    below
FOR EVER on gigantic hearts of deal

Perspective
        stars
              O Make Me
Let Me Take Me Now For
                  nothing but
gab
    And Ever
        Fade

                The girls
flow into line
        kick flurry splay
with such
        she nearly that time
                    ease
reveals invites defies
            And That Was
With a Vocal by   THE END

    :Suppose it were! to merely play
possessing what to long for, long to—all
how intimately far away.
The need to take, hurt, bind, make
love to, siphoned off
                    !Glass wall

like we too often love through anyway.

Undressing

                  reflectively
your so much more
implicit subtle tidal
           body
with such weighed awareness
of its crying sway
           my love
a crinkly stirring in the testicles
my need
        your fool
                while pondering, wise
your hitched and pinned encumbrances
let loose and weigh
            :let go
with straddled urgencies out scald
entire and salt my bleak lubricity
grip, rinse me in all asking giving
as we synchronise
                !our funny genitals

Paradise Affirmed

If we could
        only we
could only
take each other
in mid
      !air

a twining weightless
rhetoric of random
copulatives multiplying
round in under through
like threading wind
and penetrating
entire as light through
light through light

instead of this
impeded pelvic syntax
leg arm getting hold lock
ball and socket
grammar of weight and mattress
conjugal

        —we would have turned
into those naughty
meta-venereal angels
'not tied or manacled
in joint or limb'

who were in no position at all
to appreciate bone and flesh
in all the straining
luxury of limitation
reaching finding trying
timing crying for the mere
glory of organism

all but knowing how this
feels to each other
to you other to
me other
      to have the better
of both worlds
by being somewhere
forkily here between the two

      then to float up to sleep
      such sleep such
      temporary vindicated
      bodily oblivion

of substance.

Up in the where

            in a present untense
            unlike where you and I
            down in this mostly
            insufficient
            love lose alter die

He
ever since
the scapegods whom
in turn he supersedes
listens rebukes does justice to
forgives

            by definition—
            given such qualities
            as down in this
            wear quickest by
            attrition

He, far too
or too far to
care, or if, disputably;
remote from our forthcoming
genocidal spree.

Lie down love as the light
thins down
and laugh to teach us how

                (up in the
                metaphored inane
                He and the writ large
                predeceased
                illegibly
)

    while down in this
    you and I
    but not for long
    for now
    is largely why

North

   I

Grey slow-jaw comes
home to roost
at Blackhall Rocks
consuming shift by shift the dead
men huddled near the winding-shed.

Fluorescence
weeps the streets
of Pity Me
:next year's children to the soundless
piper throng the recreation ground.

Caesar's joiners
nailed the stairs
at Peterlee
my craftsman father climbed to meet the saw
toothed maker with the slow grey jaw.

See-saw, swing, and
roundabout
at Seaham Harbour
heave and whirl, a swarming tide
piped into the slag mountain side.

Under a callous
crust the pit heap
smoulders
:piper, pipe a song to learn
to walk on singing till we burn.

II *Miners' Gala*

Fancy hats and purple tights
umpteen abreast and buttocky
caper before a banner trimmed
with black for this year's dead

To publish fading banns between
Keir Hardie and a Grecian queen
swaying to the slow drum roll
and labelled Justice on a scroll.

The bands blare past into my head
and in my hand the chilly hand
of whom I was who followed some
bad piper from the promised land
to where that phrase tells lies of it.

Full wagons from the engine yard
pull empty wagons up the slow
two-mile incline from dock to pit.

III

And up and crew the grey
squall morning when I set my face
to kneel important on the verge of laughter
blessing my mother's father back to where
I saw and look in vain to see
the bedsore dead stand singing in their grave.

Sick Visit: Edges and Purposes

As we talk on about anything else
as if it were obscene

it slithers edgewise up the shelving
carpet edge as if discreetly
stalk-eyed, slow, obsequious

and flops there baleful, home among
rock sockets, fronds, and drowning trees
repeated every such and such

in patterns of obscure malignity

:its pincers flex, the hairy hind limbs
scrabble to get a grip on tilted, shifting
ledges torn with juts and snarls

on which my head splits open, spills,
and there I rummage like a crab
sidling through epitaphs and sepulchres

till, ten years old, I dream appalled
of rock slopes crawling with stone
heads that glare malignantly

(what did they mean to say?)

leaving abraded silence, in which I
shuffle my feet, edge sideways,
rake the fire, look at my hands

:blur-edged with its persistent trace
of wispy cloud, a slow bruise
climbs my nail from some

forgotten hurt; and thus I cannot keep
my mind on rituals the sick expect,
some less intense inconsequence

:the unsick can afford to ravel

patterns in the dye and weave of pain
obscurely soothed by half a sense
that all are made and undone by design

—aesthetic anaesthetic, by which I
confuse my own and your distress
and chase blurred images across the gap

:hurt egotism warms its writing hand
at fires in which tomorrow die
you, today and far too often I

in whom words breed and sidling crawl
through seascapes more abstrusely me
than manifestly mine

:through tendril frond and tree
cold firelight scribbles on the paper wall
transcribing an impossible

prolific formal botany,
leaves x-ray-veined,
a creeper geometrically

sinuous, its arcs and frequencies
the metric wave-lengths of some rarely
visible heroic singing

rising up over and under
this murderous lucent sea
through thickening vague thunder

to fall a trance of loving knowing
here between you and between me

In the prompt afterwards

of a cremation, sick of pious, kind
routine condolences
I dug a turf up in my head

and built a fire of thorny twigs
gone dry enough to raise a pungent
question mark of smoke

but came back with my mind ablaze
hearing the root's blind-sighted search,
the sliced worm's cry

:and that set fire to a rick
that burned into a space in which
an answer might have been

but vapour trails from where to roared
grew quiet wide and indistinct
like that vague rising why

: I kicked the ashes here and there
and tried to fill my head with some
less draughty emptiness

but legless horses hovering
above low frosty midnight mist
prevent my finding what

: I reach out a blind crying hand
and some old worm of terror bites it
off at the wrist

Reminded

of you propped up against the headboard
gazing through
thickening sea-fret curtain lace
at white knife-wing and awl-beak

scavenging for scraps and rinds
on rain-pooled mossy shed-roofs
no distance inland
as gull flies, albatross, ill wind,
from that encroaching abstract sea

:dead father, it reminded me
of you full twenty years ago
calling me names
for standing there ten minutes at a time

on quaking splinter-legs, too cold
to just plunge in
and save what self-esteem I could
trying, at least, to learn to swim

:and how you died, how far beyond
our equalling,
full of concern for us worn through
to see you parch and dwindle on
that bad wide sea

:and that you even said
with knife and bradawl in your chest
'O happy living things'
as wing and beak fought for the scraps

—my shouting with your anger at my son
must have reminded me,
salt kind ghost, angry as I often am
through looking forward retrospectively

Sometimes retrospection yields

little better than a haze
of countless unentire betrayals
by me, of me and of what might have been,
of those who had a right to better.

Misty negatives,
regret, remorse, unfocused
guilt, much thumbed and peered into
:too drab or true for black and white
they lie loose interleaved
between blank pages where the care
-fully mounted album peters out.

Such windows half elucidate
my never having paid
for what was never offered as a loan;
dishonoured trust; a son's exuberance
too sharply silenced;
wounded affection trifled with
to gratify a dilettantist whim;
subtle contempt bent as a shield
against love's importunities;
unaudited adjustments made
for show, for arrogance, for spite,
between the private and the public sectors
of that confused economy, the Self.

And many panes are probably lost
or scrapped, or stowed away
to tumble out afresh
when shelves spill over at the touch
of echo, family reverse, grief,
unacknowledged anniversaries.

But what is more to fear, the safe
composure of maturity
if that means gazing through
glass intricately frosted thick
as if each decade's glazed opacity
gave like Ancient Lights upon
what can't be simply bought or found
:exemplary, serene, ripe landscapes
bright with all seasonable accomplishment.

Now Showing

Thirty years later, still too soon
The Nazi Rise And Fall
                        :newsreels exhume
with gloating loathing jobbed into the track
the discomposing dead of Oradour,
Auschwitz and Lidice, Cologne

:obscenely finite images
engross and violate
each on his huddled own
in musty fetid flickering

until the front-row stalls
snigger and howl as one their fathers' age
stark, knuckle-groined, cadaverous,
quaintly composed and dignified

submits his taper decency
to squirts of liberators' DDT
which could not disinfect these who

jack-booted, naked, callous, raw
watching and doing and done to

gibe at the funny monkey in this
                                flea-pit zoo
where their forced laughter rings too true

Child's Play

Successfool beeskneesmen
make plastic (bombs perhaps
and) models in Hong Kong

of both US and Russian and
wop infantry and mortar crews
which will not last too long

for all the striking difference
between the snarling others and
the clean upstanding good

sent into war against their better
selves by honeyed man
-aging directitude

which knows how unpolitical
it would be to play soldiers with
one's own side's motives nude

and how the upshot of such trade
would be to maim the sale of toys
before the liquidation of

such men, such sons, such boys

Very Portent Impersons

interviewed on doomy runways
from-ing to in windy
cockhorse Pegasusurrus

bode a wordage languish
indistant urgent noises

ipsedicting gibberizing miserating
scyllaboom charybdis
woes of avid gullibles who

turn them up down on and off
as they down up turn off and on

:parrotty frayed owlish raven doves
gut-beaked with lie-blown
sensical half-untruth

Niet Wham

Shalt not, nor shall we not sir
render the shouldbled of our
all Umurrkn boys in
vain before the onrush of the

commun enema: their sacrivice
committed on this massive scale
for years for liberty for
decayeds of Umurrkns stillun

born and yetun dead
bears down upon Um
urrkn mothers soonun
fertilized by seed gone wrong

from the Detergent which to date
we have not nor we shall not
use unless until not under
stood perforce we come to over

kill against our will of
God and right against the left
if anything is left at all

:Umurrknamese and Ho Chi Sam
confounded in the great Inflam

In War Time

I

The only buds
(but far too big
even if they were leaves,
and it is bleak December)

stand out as if appalling
rumour had swelled, sprouted
heart-shaped through gnarled
thick bark

black lumps of grief
the heart's mutations
after some ruinous defoliant—
the only buds

are stiff big brooding crows
swelled mutely through the twilight
on the sly

a terrible ugly is born.

Settled in for keeps
perched there incongruous, exotic
charred stiffs
from what far bonfire

—bad news, bad napalm—
they seem not to relate
to what this wintry weather
equally provides

over the distant copse
(vague purple skyline, igneous)
rippling writhes and thickenings
as of black smoke

all that is become of
minutes ago the thunderous
wings wild crying intense
concert of reavement—

thousands of starlings
gathered to migrate
taking their bearings
up off the stubbly dry

up off the barren branches
punctual, mysteriously oriented . . .

Swarmings of smoky newsprint
:U.S. Alone In Search For Peace
Vietcong Atrocities
and, easily ignored,

Peace Delegates To Asia
seasonable, daring to take
heed, the priceless, practically
useless non-strategic immaterial

leaving me feeling cheaply
occidental, choosing the right side
(feelings are a western privilege)
compassionate in battles
fought far off

and fought ostensibly by both
sides in the name of values
each one claims the other violates
and most of them I honour
when I dare

but far too ready to forget
these sprouting charcoal crows
could symbolize, as well
as Asian heroes turned to coal,

less palpable, that worser cautery
Abe Lincoln's late cremators
burning their ideals
in black fires for the sake of

Freedom General Motors Peace

—framed heroes, like most heroes
like the peasants burned, and like
most heroes blind, naive
stone-hearted, ardent, brilliant

or one or more of these,
dead as no causes quite deserve,
live as no causes quite deserve,
the chain gangs of events—

and far too ready to forget
the worst that can be said
against America is being said
and shouted and placarded,
urinated on the walls of power

and cheapened in its turn
by necessary violence,
banners, labels, mirror motives,
by themselves, Americans, the upstaged

darlings of grandpappy Europe

so that they will never be
for us to patronize again
and ought to understand
if ever, now, the priceless

asset an imperial record is
and for the world to fear

the altruistic lies, evangelisms,
fire absurd allegiance
martyrdom fire stupid fire
hypocrisy fire shining fire life

death mess mess mess.

While at this distance, wintry,
swells the half-true, disabling
sense 'the whole affair'
is tragically necessary

in deeper human terms than

'economic laws'
'political impasse'
'ideological confrontation'
and other swank astrologies

mess mess mess mess.

Knowing it so, take sides
for what it costs us
(which is most of why)
—all sides are specious clarities

and most as ignorant as you, as I,
whether close to the fire
or in the spuriously
tolerable afterglow

in England, curiously
wise in such old ignorances,
tender of conscience, shifty
slave of Wall Street and the dollar

migrant-hearted, little,
wintering with crows.

II *Parade*
We say we care
do I? you do—it's fashionable
to, or seem to, for far
everybody, and to take the right

left side, left right, quick
march, Opinion! drilled by
well-prosed instructioners
who put a face of glassy bright

impervious concern
on squads of issues of high
audience rating—crudify!
'then can you tell us in one

word what you consider should be—?'
left right rhubarb left

left righteousness,
let us condemn one side outright
for thinking only
one side right

:David Slings Discriminate Grenades.

Militant pacifists!
come let us boil
discussion up
to boil it down—

encapsulate!
bring badges mottoes mumbos jumbos
tear up, shoot down
in the name of loving, hate!

Goliath Is A Texas Philistine.

Ill liberal humorists!
defoliate all ancient trees
with mists of self-absolving
fascunable mockery

let glare strike through
to fertilize the stunted
undergrowth, let sprout
let parrot shout

lurv lurv lurv lurv
sweet self-struck anarch, prophesy!
'We reject history, unlike our
predecessors.'

Newscaster, fish us quick
a kippered Asiatic,
feast our eyes on smoked yellow
fillets from Da Nang—

we surfeit comfortably
on sudden bright
impressions of disaster, grow fat
eating flies, we thrive

on distant carrion caw caw
a just war is just war.

As twilight thickens mutely
on the sly, outside, beyond us,
lighten our darkness with your
very latest early warnings

but teach us caring
should be careful,
mockery a wounded last resort,
apocalypse no shallow bright remark

dissent no intellectomy,
error no egg to crow about

love something terrible
to do with daring,
daring the decorated slave
of chains of tragic error

:Freedom Self-Determination Peace

high values warped for banner
headlines, lying press release,
incendiary pious
rhubarb rhubarb rhubarb—

why print David's version
if Goliath lines your purse?
'Just then flew by a monstrous crow . . .'

III *Envoy*

A carrion crow sat on an oak
(sing hi there, carrion crow)
smallish man-size, black with smoke
from the Noise of America, ho.

They brought it back to Disneyland
to hop about and squawk
apocalypsos through the movie
Tweedle Brothers, Chum and chi

Or, Eek's Defeat Of Orc.

Tell William Blake his hero
fights like crazy until
the Statue of Liberty
knocks him flat

bang pow aargh oof kersplat.

A carrion crow sat on an oak
(night is drawing nigh)
fire-tongued pterodactyls
steal across the sky—

Orc and his million
manifest Asians
baked in a pie!

So simply tapped

so ludicrously
indiscriminate
unusable

this desperate high
silent crying
:does it

steadily secrete
build up against
no matter what

pretence, responsibility,
habit or more filmy
membrane

is it plenitude

to spill out so
from far back in among
dark dark

all brinks and verges
flooded by simple
accident

the touch of
obsolete endearments
trashy songs

need need need need

as if life were mere
random floodings of a
drained lake bed

surging from deep
reservoirs of lack
or fear

:too true, and nowhere nearly
true enough, for all that cry
insists

a deadly night shades into
everything—but why is
hollowness so full

so unappeased fulfilment
so incomparably
eloquent

this crying speechless
puzzlingly
serene?

Far Cry

Given this who knows why
seventy years wide breathing space
man wishful fills it with a face
and out of earshot his far cry
reverberates, while he
beside himself with wishing, hears
the far-fetched music of the spheres
utter responses reassuringly

:we guess whom we address
(three guesses make a trinity)
and whom we name
to calm our crying shame
we choose at random, cannot hope
unless beyond all hope to know
where unless nowhere our loud murmurs go
(three murmurs haunt infinity)

The Powers that Be

Eyes that see
(said the blind man)
bandaged up the bright
misleading stare of morning
that I might see in the night.

Silence, dumb
(yelled the deaf man)
to any ears but these,
whispers in my shell the secrets
of its arcane seas.

Hands of sky
(signed the dumb man)
gesture night and day,
and my ten talking fingers
interpret what they say.

Powers that be
(mocked the mad man)
laugh to hear their cries,
knowing an itch for wholeness
tickles their holy lies.

Make me mad
(said the whole man)
dumb and deaf and blind
:truths I hanker after
the maimed and wretched find.

Philosophy

One, with a burden on his mind
of This-ness, thinks 'I Am'
:denying image (each tree is each tree)
stands in an unreflecting void
bruises his eyes with vividness
and cannot see for looking.

One, with a clear view (like the blind)
of Elsewhere, thinks 'I shall become'
:asserting image (all trees make a wood)
kneels in a consecrated mist
closes his eyes for tidiness
and cannot look for seeing.

Wise fools, foolish wise
:but what of sober common sense
secure between two stools
who from its peg takes down the world
regardless of the cosmic rules
and tries it on for size?

What right has who to talk of fools?

Home Thoughts from Toronto

    I
'Read all about it'
              Blind News Vendor
                                      yells
weighing a nickel of the
                      Ten Billion Dollars
I read half about
                To Be Earned In The Next
decayed
        By The Developed Countries
Through The Sale Of Arms
                            eyes legs hands limbs

which little per cent interests
blind civic stares
through Summerhill Queen Union King
the stations of the
                well-kempt underworld
invested in blue light
                as if these
Go Ahead People
        were to
Make One Hundred Out Of Every Seventy-Five
                                      dolours

II
What is she doing, at her time of
!live, with wilfully glazed eyes
among besuited these unsuitable
bland beeskneesmen
                  as if she were
                              (she is
irresistible to look at and as if
their seedy glances violate
                        (they do
her dreaming
              Maybe The Real You Is A Blonde?

III
'As we push farther north
                        the tourists
are right in there behind the
                            bulldozers'
in wicked Sam's low swinging chariots.

Gratis à l'intérieur
                      bilingual Kellogg promises
animal sauvage
            of plastic, wrapped
like nearly every thing, in
paper, polythene, praise, purity
                        Now Wash Your Hands

Ontario, the soil! the air
                  -conditioned
cottagey Interior! the rooted maple fires!

IV
'They half expect *us* to learn
                    French!'

      Sweet nervous Anglo-Saxons
                      bless those
English-piquing
             frogs poles eyeties krauts
who shall inherit
             a left wing some day
no queen but maybe
                 some blithe President

:of France?
        (that scared you

  V *Girl Number Twenty*
             'we are desirous to explain
             the philosophy of our school
             and your child's place in it'
to raise her down into informity
sweetness and trite

Define A
        (strawberry sauvage non-conformist
MOOSE
        (and written on its brow
one hundred lines
           I Must Be Good
for crossing its i's

  VI
Those college birds at Guelph
allowed to major in
             Poultry Science
and in latin
      minor

should make the goose that laid
                 the syllabus
translate that cackle on the Capitol
when his ancestral Goths
           flopped
hopefully up the hill.

VII

Hooked on pot above a camp
-fire stoked by hippy middle
-aging peepsters diag
-nosing into black mass
-media and the yellow press

'The ailments of our culture'
                              puff puff
'teenage problem'
which raucous these wool-gathering
victims of lysergic acid
may survive, outgrow
                        no thanks to punditry
but in what thriving light
of subtler rhythms and what
deeper soil
           concerns me near, not being yet
and I hope not
              this side of three score years or so
more cold than hot
              puff puff

'the younger generation'
                        promotional sweethearts
of this vast gilt incontinent

VIII

The lift up to the doctor's suite
plays music as of harps
                to greet
or bid farewell
              and sweetens the imagination with
and ounce of civet
            :Primitif?
Clean Living? (The Real Safeguard)

But I am sweaty Kubla Khan
before whose merely tread
the supermarket doors fling wide
sweet corny promises
on floating sanitized mattresses
of music
        canned

Hello. . .Testing

Trying to memorize a sky
some other how than in the words
we see it through and freeze it by

—poetic justice! icicled
light-years burned into the head

 :unsayable certainly feels, close to,
unlike not-hitherto-said